The Habit Hacker
Seven steps to break damaging habits and create healthy habits to increase your success

The Habit Hacker
Copyright © 2018 Clarity Cove Publishing/ CreateSpace Publishing

All Rights Reserved. No part of this book can be scanned, distributed or copied without permission.

Foreword by LisaBeth Willis

Interior Design by Nicolya Williams

For more information email Nicolya@nicolyawilliams.com

For every woman who is tired of dreaming about success, but ready to make it happen!

Dedication

This book is dedicated to my two beautiful daughters Kaelyn and Kamryn. You two are my biggest blessings!

Acknowledgments

To my Savior: You have taken the dark place I was in planted and grown me in ways I was not even aware was possible. For the pain that developed my purpose, I thank you. Lord, you are omnipotent and amazing. I love you and honor you ALWAYS!

Kaelyn: When I found out I was going to be a mom, nobody could have ever prepared me for the blessings you would and continue to bring to my life. You are such a sweet soul with so much dedication and love. You have the biggest heart and you're always focused on God. You are so smart and innovative. You're amazing and I truly mean that. I pray that never changes. I love you princess!

Kamryn: Becoming your mother was one of the best blessings of all of my life. Kami you are such an amazing little girl. I love your creativity, your willingness to try something new and your perseverance. On the days when I only want to cry, you remind me to stay strong. On the days when I am too serious, you remind me why I need to laugh. Every day I learn something new from you and it inspires me. I love you baby!

Welcome to *The Habit Hacker*. This book was designed to help you diagnose your unhealthy habits and replace them with habits that will put you on the path to succeed. In this book, you will learn a simple strategy to challenge those habits that have prevented you from living the life and being the person you truly aspire to be.

Time to initiate lasting change…

Table of Contents

Foreword 7
Introduction 9
Chapter 1: So, What Are Habits? 15
Chapter 2- It All Begins In Your Mind 19
Chapter 3 - Bring Awareness 27
Chapter 4- What Is Your Why? 31
Chapter 5- Begin Today 35
Chapter 6- Believe in Yourself 39
Chapter 7- Getting Accountability 45
Chapter 8 - Facing Your Fear 51
Chapter 9 - Give Grace 55
Chapter 10 - Visualize The Outcome 59
Chapter 11- Being Courageous 63
Chapter 12 - Conclusion 67
My habits lead to goal achievement. 70

Foreword

By: LisaBeth Willis- Author and Publisher

Nicolya Williams first caught my attention as a member of a private Facebook group led by our mutual life coach. Nicolya had responded to a post and mentioned she was in Columbus, Ohio, which is about an hour east of where I reside in Dayton. It did not take long for me to notice her going "live" with her daily inspiration. I was very impressed not only with her apparent drive and motivation, but with the passion with which she articulated conversation with viewers. It was very apparent that she not only loved encouraging others to action, but also that she cared about the work she was implementing.

When Nicolya contacted me to request that, I write the foreword to *The Habit Hacker*, I responded with an immediate "yes," as I was confident that this project would potentially help millions. As an author and speaker, it is my desire to share wisdom with others and it was obvious that this was a trait that Nicolya and I shared. *The Habit Hacker* explores everyday practices that can be implemented to create change both on a personal level and in the greater environment. Nicolya begins by encouraging readers to begin with the foundation of mindset change and cites expert opinions to support her assertions.

Her declarations are thorough as she outlines steps to create a lifestyle that leads to personal and professional achievements. She also includes tips and introspective questions that are designed for readers to examine themselves at their current level and leads them directly to a triumphant path. Regardless of career, readers will find a roadmap to success in *The Habit Hacker*. In addition, the workbook at the end includes a calendar style habit tracker that can be used as a tool to support readers in their new lifestyle. Overall, Nicolya does an excellent job ensuring that each paragraph is easy to read and easy to implement. As a full-time employee and author entrepreneur, time management is paramount and I look forward to implementing some of the tools that are shared in this amazing book.

Introduction

"Motivation is what gets you started. Habit is what keeps you going."
~Jim Ryun

In my role as a personal development coach, I decided to do some market research calls. I wanted to talk with women to see what are some of the biggest barriers that prevent them from achieving their goals. The women with whom I spoke identified procrastination as a primary reason. They also identified fear, which was rooted in a ton of different things. Through the conversations I had, I noticed that many of these women struggled with making decisions on a day-to-day basis. Although they often failed to notice it or avoided admitting it, these women were making seemingly small decisions that was making a huge impact on their life. The worst part is that they were not always aware that this was taking place.

After speaking with these women, I knew this was a topic that I needed to address in order to bring awareness to other women all across the world. You see, many people do not recognize the impact that their daily choices have on their life. The truth is our choices compound. If you want to lose weight but you make unhealthy food choices every day, it will in turn have a negative impact on your weight. Drinking soda in moderation is not bad, but if you drink it daily it will definitely add up. On the reverse side, if you want to write a book and decide to spend 15 minutes per day writing, that does not seem like a lot. However, when you add 15 minutes each day that is a total of almost two hours at the end of the week. At the end of a month, that is approximately seven to eight hours. Take it from me; you can get a lot written within that time period.

One of the things I noticed when I did my market research calls was that women were saying they did not realize the impact of what seemed to be small habits. That which begins small will compound itself. For example, if you want to lose weight, but every day you eat one honey bun, you probably will not lose much weight. However, if you eat one honey bun once per week, having that moderation will contribute to better weight loss. Understand that when bad habits compound, it counteracts what you are trying to accomplish. The same thing happens with good habits. If you decide to spend more time reading God's word and you start to consistently study for a specific amount of time, you will increase your knowledge of The Word as a result.

As I worked to learn more, about the women, I spoke with and the habits that were highlighted, I found that they were not dedicating enough time building their businesses. The most common distraction was television. They were spending way too much time watching TV. They shared how they had often fallen short with other goals in order to do what was comfortable and familiar. They revealed that they struggled with finding time for self-care and how overall, they were exhausted and miserable. These women had various habits that were affecting their success in subtle ways. In doing this research, I realized how many women really needed this message and that is what has inspired me to write this book.

Before you dig into this, I want you to think about a habit that you have that you believe has a negative impact on your life. I know mine is my sweet tooth. I have a terrible addiction to sweets. They are my downfall! I have worked very hard over the last year to really change this addiction and I will let you in on the secret. In order to overcome this bad habit, I started tracking my eating patterns and replacing sweets with healthier options. Now, I have not been perfect. Sometimes I fail too, but I have been able to pinpoint a strategy that has positively changed my progress and made it possible to handle that weakness. In my experience, I came to realize that breaking bad habits is not for the faint of heart and that in using this strategy it made it much more possible to overcome.

Mark Twain says it best: "Nothing so needs reforming as other people's habits." This quote is what inspired me to help women reform their habits by sharing this information. Before you go on to read the remainder of this book, I have identified some things that you will need in order to be successful. First, I need you to read this book with both an honest and open mind. If you remain closed minded or offended you will not learn how to master your daily actions and in turn master the outcome of your life. One of my favorite quotes is "Do what is right not what is easy." This quote can be applied to many situations, but for this book, I really felt it was appropriate. I know that the choices we make are often the easy choices. They are what is comfortable and what we are accustomed to. They provide us with peace and security because we have become familiar with them. The truth is they also keep us limited or stuck and they keep us from growing and reaching our potential. That is why it is important to do what is right even if it is NOT easy. When we identify a habit we need to develop or break, it is usually because we know it is the right thing to do. When we do the right thing there are a number of results that could come into fruition that otherwise may not have manifested. It could include personal growth, imparting inspiration to others, reaching goals that seemed too far-fetched and increasing your self-confidence, just to name a few.

Your quality of life is directly affected by your habits. Most people with high energy make daily choices to rest and nourish their body with water and healthy foods. People who are rich often spend time investing in their understanding of money as well as into their businesses. Intelligent people spend time reading and learning. Their quality of life is determined by the choices that they make. Now that we know our habits determine our life and success, there is nothing more important than making it a priority to master your habits. This will have a major impact on your life.

The next thing I need for you to do is reflect on what your habits are and in turn, be willing to confront the habits that need to change. At the end of each chapter, there will be an opportunity to reflect on your habits as well as the impact of those habits and the changes you desire to make. Do not rush through this process. You got this book because you want lasting change. In order to make that happen you have to go through the process and be able to learn through your reflection time. I am a big advocate for reflection because it has changed my life.

Here are three main benefits of reflection:

Reflection helps you learn from your mistakes. If we do not reflect on our mistakes and choices, we are destined to repeat them. Obviously, that is not what we want and it is not very smart. However, if we take time to reflect on those mistakes, figure out what went wrong and see how we can prevent them in the future, we can then use our mistakes to get better. Mistakes and failures become a valuable learning tool instead of something to feel embarrassed or upset about. Reflection is an important way to do that.

Reflection enables you to get new ideas. When I reflect on things that I am working on or things that are going on in my life, I trigger the creative side of my brain. It inspires me to take more creative action to make the changes needed. Honestly, many of my business and book ideas were born during times of personal reflection.

Reflection gives you perspective. We are often caught up in the troubles or busy-ness of our daily lives. All of the tasks we have to complete can seem to overwhelm us, and then we lose sight of the big picture and what truly matters. When we take time to reflect, it can calm us, lower our stress levels and help us to realize that our problems are not that big after all. It really gives us perspective and that is a good thing.

    You grabbed this book because you are ready to make the changes in your life to reach your potential. While I can give you all of the information in the world, if you do not apply it, it will be pointless. Take this information and use it. Your life matters, your goals and success are very important, so live as though you know that.

Reflection
"The more reflective you are, the more effective you are."
~Hall and Simeral

- When trying something new it is important that you set intentions for the journey. Take a moment and ask yourself: What are you hoping to gain from this book?

- Do you believe that your habits have played a role in the quality of your life? How so?

- Do you agree to be honest and reflect regularly throughout the process of reading this book?

- If so, how will you maintain your consistency with that?

Chapter 1: So, What Are Habits?

"99% of Failures come from people who have the habit of making excuses."
~George Washington Carver

Let us begin by defining habits. Habits are a regular practice that are difficult to break. It has been said that the quality of our lives is determined by our habits. Most people form habits without knowing the impact that they are going to have. The quality of life is determined by the patterns or the habits that we develop. The tricky part about habits is that they usually feel good or are somewhat familiar and therefore they seem normal. For example, you may go to happy hour every day on your way home from work because it is on your route. This does not necessarily seem bad until you begin to reflect on the other areas of your life that it is affecting such as your finances or being on time to pick up your children. It is not until you get tired of the process or recognize the troubles that it causes that you are in a position to change the habit for good.

When you are trying to get rid of a habit, the first few days are difficult and it may seem impossible to break the habit. This is because you have made the habit a norm. It is part of your comfort zone, and we all know how challenging it is to break free from your comfort zone. The truth is, real freedom and growth is outside the zone of comfort. The key to breaking habits all begins with your mindset. Who we are and what we accomplish depends largely on a vast network of routines and behaviors that we carry out with little to no thought each day.

How Habits Are Formed

When we first begin a new task, our brains are working hard to process the new information we are learning. As soon as we understand how a task works, the behavior becomes automatic. The mental activity required to do the task decreases dramatically. Habits are the brain's own internal productivity drivers. As it is constantly striving for more efficiency, the brain quickly transforms as many tasks and behaviors as possible into habits so that we can do them without thinking, thus freeing up more brainpower to tackle new challenges. Bad habits go unnoticed. Removing them is often more important than developing good ones. Bad habits, if unchecked, encroach on the good ones.

In <u>The Power of Habit: Why We Do What We Do in Life and Business</u>, writer Charles Duhigg states, "This process—in which the brain converts a sequence of actions into an automatic routine—is known as 'chunking,' and it is at the root of how habits form. There are dozens—if not hundreds—of behavioral chunks that we rely on every day." One good example would be driving. Take a moment and think about how much brainpower and concentration you had to use the first time you learned to drive your car. Now compare that to the amount of mental effort you exert when you are driving today. If you are anything like me I don't even remember driving most of the time, which is a completely different thing.

David Eagleman writes in *Incognito*, "Brains are in the business of gathering information and steering behavior appropriately. It does not matter whether consciousness is involved in the decision-making. And most of the time, it's not." That is how habits work on a loop. First, there is a cue, also known as a trigger, that tells your brain to go into automatic mode and which habit to use. Then, there is the routine, which can be physical, mental or emotional. This is something you have developed in the time you were forming the habit. Lastly, there is a reward, which in turn helps your brain figure out if this particular loop is worth remembering for the future. Over some time, this habit loop becomes automatic. The cue and reward become intertwined with each other until a powerful sense of anticipation emerges.

This is the very reason habits become addictive. Our brains are wired to do them automatically and there is usually a reward we get that inspires our brain to remember that for next time. This is why it is so important to break down the habit process so that you can create a strategy to overcome them effectively.

Reflection
"The more reflective you are, the more effective you are."
~Hall and Simeral

- Do you believe that you have more *good* habits than *bad* habits?

- Do you believe that who you are is primarily determined by your habits?

- What three habits do you have of which you are the most proud?

- What are three habits that you wish you didn't have?

Chapter 2- It All Begins In Your Mind

"The number one habit of successful people is to foster a growth mindset." –Unknown

Nothing is more important than a changed mind. Not what you are wearing, your hairstyle, your nail color, your house or your car. Many people assume that an outward change equates to a mindset shift and that could not be further from the truth. For example, on New Year's, people come up with many great ideas. They believe that they will do things like work out more, get more sleep or read more. You may see some of the following hashtags online: #Newyearnewme, #changed and #thisismyyear among others. You may even find people shouting out their goals as a status stating "I am going to stop eating junk foods" or "I'm going to stop watching so much TV," only to fail at implementing that new habit within a few weeks. Based on statistics generated about New Year's resolutions, most people have given up on their goals by January 12th. In fact, January 12th is called National Quitter's Day for that reason. People begin to slide back into their old habits. Before you know it, they are back to their old patterns and routines. This is not because they were lying; it is not even, because they did not really want it. They have these ideas, they even have the desire behind it, but they do not have a plan to ensure that they can make it happen. Not having a strategy is what seems to be the key contributor to falling short on reaching your goals.

A few years ago on New Year's Day, I convinced my mother to join the gym. She had been complaining about her weight, but was not a very active person. I knew that if I were with her it would help her to stay more consistent. The first week we were at the gym it was packed with people. I told my mother to watch the number of people decline as the weeks go by. Sure enough, by the end of January the gym was close to being empty again. The consistent people came, but none of the new enrollees. My belief is that all of those individuals had set New Year's resolutions, but were not doing anything about creating a plan to implement new healthy habits and rid themselves of poor familiar habits.

As you are working to identify the habits that you want to break, make sure you also identify what that looks like for you. Therefore, if you want to start working out but have never had a consistent workout regimen, which could mean starting with working out for 15 minutes per day. That may not seem like a lot to some people, but that is HUGE for you since you had not done that previously. If you say, you will stop watching so much television, maybe you begin by cutting back by thirty minutes a day. That may seem miniscule, but if you are accustomed to watching television for hours, that is a challenge. For some of you, the habit you're working on breaking may be spending too much money. Instead of buying Starbucks five days a week, you can reduce it down to three. When you do it that way, you are not spending as much money, which aligns with your financial discipline goal. For every individual, breaking habits will look different.

If you want anything in life, you must first conquer your mind; you must have a change in your mindset. You see, so many of us get so accustomed to the patterns we develop and the thought processes that happen in our mind that we don't even realize how impactful they are in our lives. Have you ever heard the quote "Whether you believe you can or you can't, you're probably right?" The statement is true because we believe what we internalize. If we believe that we can, we can. If we believe that we can't, we cannot. With breaking or beginning habits, you must believe that you are capable of accomplishing it. If you set these goals and fail to believe that it will ever happen, it will not. If you believe that you can accomplish your goals of breaking that bad habit in your life, you can. You just have to believe it.

So many women get comfortable and embrace those negative patterns as if they're addicted to them because they feel comfortable. They feel like the habit is protecting them when in reality, the habit is selling them short. Habits keep us stuck; they keep us limited. The bigger picture is that you must overcome those mindset patterns. I'm not promising you that it will be easy, but here I'll share with you a few tips that can help you work through overcoming those mindset patterns. You see, so many of us travel through life with our foot on the brake pedal and we wonder why we are not getting anywhere. It is because our mind is keeping us stuck. It is keeping us from going forward and pursuing our dreams because all of the thoughts that are hindering us. Before you know it, you start to believe those things. You start to internalize the negative thinking and make them part of your reality when they do not need to be.

I once had a yoga instructor tell me "If you can conquer your mind, you literally can conquer anything." See, it is so important that we first work on inward change before we can work on outward change. I can ask my clients whether they want to feel better. I can encourage them to not focus on fixing the physical aspects like your hair, your house or your car. That stuff is fun, but if we are not addressing what is happening in your mind, our efforts will be futile. Our mindset is generally unchanging without some direct and conscientious effort. Therefore, it is important that we conquer the mental roadblocks by thinking about positive things and making it work for our benefit instead of working against us. That is imperative for success.

In order to really work on that, you must first make a choice. You must choose whether you want to make a change or stay the same. It has to be an intentional choice. It needs to be because you are sick and tired of being sick and tired. It needs to be because you are sick of the mindset, thoughts and the things that are confusing you, keeping you stuck or keeping you limited. It has to be because you are sick of the habits that your mind has told you are acceptable, but deep down you realize they are hindering your success.

To conquer your mind there are a few small steps that you will need to take. The most important thing is to be consistent so that you are staying in control of your thoughts. The first step is that you must decide that you want to be bigger than your thoughts. You must decide that you want to conquer those negative thought patterns and habits. I have one strategy that has helped to redirect my negative thinking. I call it the "but rule." We often tell ourselves negative things that we come to believe. Instead of embracing the negative, change it up. When you begin to say negative things, follow them up with *but* followed by a positive statement. For example, you may say to yourself, "I eat too much and now I'm fat." Instead of stopping there and feeling discouraged, you could chose to say "I eat so much and now I'm fat, but if I start changing my eating habits today I can be healthier within a few months." On the other hand, you may say to yourself, "I spend too much money. I'm never going to be able to go on vacation." You could follow up and say, "I spend too much money and I feel like I'm never going to be able to go on that trip, but if I stop buying fast food every day that will push me closer to my goal." This may seem like a silly strategy, but it has been amazing for me. I did not realize how many thoughts I had internalized and allowed to become my reality. Trying this concept allowed me to put my thoughts back in my control and make them more positive.

The second step would be to surround yourself with positive people. I realized I had spent a lot of time surrounded by pessimists. Those "glass-half empty" people who never see anything good and never believe that change is possible. I had to change that and I am sharing with you how important it is to surround yourself with people who have a more positive outlook. The way they live and think will pour over into your life, helping you to improve your mindset.

Finally, the third step is not accepting negativity from anybody. You do not have to believe what somebody told you. You do not have to listen to bad things; it is your job to embrace the positivity. You do not need any more negativity in your life. Your job is to surround yourself with people who will be positive as well as to continuously rid yourself of negative people. I once had a teacher tell me that I was a horrible writer. For years, I embraced what she said as truth and it stopped me from wanting to write, do blogs and video blogs. It stopped me from wanting to finish school as well. When I changed my mind and decided that no longer had to be the truth I was embracing, it changed my life.

Challenge every negative thought by replacing it with a positive thought or statement. Every time you say or believe "I'm not qualified" follow that thought up with "Wow! I accomplished this!" Or "Wow! I am brave enough to even think of this idea." Every time you give yourself reasons why you cannot start new habits or break old ones, challenge yourself to identify the reasons why you should and why you can. You can even take it a step further and challenge all thoughts. For every negative thought, practice two positive thoughts. You are going to be shocked at how many times a day you have to do this. Oftentimes we do not even know that these thoughts are coming because we have just become so accustomed to them. When you choose to cover negative thoughts with positive ones, it will change your life. Before you realize it, you will have created a new healthy habit for yourself.

There is so much power in conquering your mind if you just embrace it and work on it a little bit at a time. The truth is, the things that you have been doing have not been effective. Give yourself permission to try something new. Give yourself permission to do some things that I have seen work for both myself as well as my clients. Believe that it is possible. It all starts with one-step in the right direction. Dr. Martin Luther King Jr. says, "Take the first step even though you may not see the whole staircase." Take the first step by changing your mind and watch how it manifests in your life.

Reflection
"The more reflective you are, the more effective you are."
~Hall and Simeral

- What is the biggest thing you need to conquer in your mind right now?

- What is the BIGGEST habit you are trying to break and what will the outcome look like for you?

- Who are the top five people you spend your time with?

- Are they adding or subtracting from your life? How so?

Chapter 3 - Bring Awareness

"Depending on what they are, our habits will either make us or break us. We become what we repeatedly do."
~Sean Covey

After addressing your mindset, the next step is to become aware of your habits. You cannot make changes in things that you avoid or run away from. Take a moment and think of the habits that define you. Maybe you watch so much TV you could name all of the episodes of *Scandal*. Maybe you are on social media so much that everyone knows that they can contact you at any hour of the day. Ask yourself whether these habits add value to your life.

We all have habits that define us in some way or another. The trouble is that the habits that define us are not necessarily good. For example, if you do know how to name all of the episodes of a particular television show, how is that pushing you closer to your goals? On the other hand, maybe working out so much prevents you from spending dinnertime with your family. It is so important that we face our habits. As a personal development coach, when I work with women the first thing we talk about is their day to day habits. Your day-to-day habits determine the course of your life. Many people try to run or avoid facing their habits because frankly, they are comfortable. Those habits are what we think works for us. We love watching TV, eating at restaurants, and going shopping. Consequently, we feeling unaccomplished when we have not saved money or do not sleep well. The truth is that we are not being honest with ourselves and fail to admit that we can sometimes be our own worst enemy. Without facing and confronting your habits, you are never going to be able to get to a place where you can make the change that you need in order to live the life you desire to live.

Now take a moment and ask yourself what you want to become. The more important question is, who do you *want* to become? What are the habits that make that person? If you want to be an artist, you need to paint every day. Do you want to be a writer? You need to have a daily writing habit. Do you want to finish a triathlon? You will need to train daily. Do you want to be a great parent? Commit to regular quality time with your kids. You get the idea.

A famous quote by Samuel Johnson states, "The chains of habit are too weak to be felt until they are too strong to be broken." You see, when we form habits we often start small and don't see the trouble in them. They begin tiny and often go unnoticed until they are too difficult to break. After all, one milkshake isn't terrible. However, when you have formed the habit of drinking five milkshakes per week, we are talking about something completely different. This can happen with any of our habits. They all start small and then they expand into something that feels completely out of our control. Once they become a normal pattern or part of your life, they become increasingly difficult to get rid of. This is why it is important to bring awareness to the habit and make a plan for change.

Reflection
"The more reflective you are, the more effective you are."
~Hall and Simeral

- What are the habits that have defined you?

- What have your habits caused you to feel?

- What or who is it that you desire to become? Be very descriptive.

Chapter 4- What Is Your Why?

"Successful people are simply those with successful habits."
~Brian Tracy

Are you embarrassed to share your habits or to engage in them in front of others? If so, that means it is time to make a change. Stephen King says "A man who can't bear to share his habits is a man who needs to quit them." I speak with women every day that have BIG life goals, but cannot bear to face the habits that are in their way. Trust me, I am not judging because I have dealt with that personally. I will give you an example. My aunt is a health coach. She went to a great school, and one of the things she shared with me is the impact of consuming dairy products. It seemed that she read those stats and facts until she turned blue in the face. Honestly, I was not ready to hear it because I love cheese. When she shared all these things with me and why I needed to get cheese out of my diet, I knew that it sounded important, but I loved cheese far too much to give it up.

A few months ago, I found out that my youngest daughter may be lactose intolerant and has been having bad reactions to dairy products. That was a life changer for me and gave me more motivation to remove dairy from my household altogether. Although I had been hearing all of this information from my aunt for years, it did not give me a strong enough *why* to make the needed change. Now I have a different reason to break my cheese eating habit. That reason is because my daughter is negatively affected by it, and she served as a strong motivating factor to make the change.

In order to break your bad habits you have to have a strong reason why you want the habit to be broken. You cannot want to break the habit because someone else told you to do that. You cannot break a habit simply because you read this book. It has to be because *you* are ready for the change and *you* are willing to put in the work.

When your "why" is something that matters to you there is more passion behind it. If you do not have that drive or that "why" behind wanting to get rid of a habit, it probably will not last. For example, maybe you want to control your spending habits because you live in a bad neighborhood and you really want to buy a new house. It could be because you want to put your children in a better school district. If you want to buy a house, you need to have that financial discipline to succeed. It may be something different for you, but you must be willing to identify that "why." It is imperative because you have to gain that momentum and get that newly formed habit implemented.

Once you identify your why you must keep that in the forefront of your mind at all times. When I began writing my first book, I remember feeling as if I wanted to give up all of the time. I wanted to fall back into the habit of watching TV or sitting on the phone or being on social media instead of writing. Honestly it would have been easier to fall back into those habits because I had made them part of my comfort zone. Each time I wanted to do that I would reflect on the reason why I was doing what I was doing. My reason was I wanted to leave a legacy for my daughters. Every time I felt tempted to fall back into my old habits, I would remember the importance of leaving a legacy and what that would mean for my girls. At one point in my writing process, I put a picture of my daughters up on my computer. That always gave me the momentum that I needed to keep going and making the change that was going to push me closer to my success.

Reflection
"The more reflective you are, the more effective you are."
~Hall and Simeral

- What is the number one reason why you want to break or add new habits to your life?

- How can you use this *why* to give you the momentum you need to move forward with success?

- How can you keep your *why* in front of you at all times?

Chapter 5- Begin Today

"The right time is any time that one is still so lucky as to have."
~ Henry James

Monday, Tuesday, Wednesday, Thursday, Friday, Saturday and Sunday. All seven days are listed and not one of them is titled "Someday." So many people are "someday thinkers" saying things such as:

"Someday I will eat better."
"Someday I will quit smoking or drinking."
"Someday I will get in the gym."
"Someday I will save money."
"Someday I will go to church regularly."

Someday, someday, someday. I hate someday thinking because it will never push you closer to your dreams. Get rid of the someday thinking. Replace the someday thinking with TODAY thinking.

When it comes time to break habits, the majority of people are waiting for the perfect moment to make the change. They say things like, "I'll start eating healthy after my birthday" or "I'll stop watching TV after the season is over" or "I will start exercising once this work project is done." I promise that if you always wait for that moment, you will not find it. There will always be an excuse to wait just a little bit longer or to hold on just a little while longer. When you do not give yourself that option and you just jump right into the process of getting rid of the habit, you put yourself in a position to succeed at breaking your habits. You remove the opportunity to give yourself excuses.

Make a non-negotiable decision to start TODAY. There will never be a perfect moment, time, date or set of circumstances for the habit that you are trying stop. When I started my healthy eating lifestyle and began minimizing sweets in my diet, I kept saying that I would wait until Sunday. Sunday is the fresh start of the week, but every Sunday I had a new excuse for why I could not do it. That got old. Then I would pick another day and remember that meant I would not be able to go to someone's gathering because I could not eat like I wanted to. There was always an excuse to not make the change. Being stuck in that cycle was torture because I was going around and around listing all of the reasons, I could not change and justifying my detrimental habits. Do you know how many weeks passed that I could have just started?

The same thing happened with my business. I kept saying that I wanted to start a business. I believed that I would start it someday when I had enough money, or someday when I gained enough confidence, or even someday when I had enough support. That just gave me excuses that continued to push me back. Those excuses kept me stuck and kept me limited. You cannot just say that *someday* you want to break them; it needs to be today. You need to make a non-negotiable decision to make today the day that you are going to start. All of the stars will never perfectly align; there will be days, moments or situations that will not work in your favor. That is okay. It is still possible to break your habits. I want to leave you with this: <u>Today is the only promised day.</u> Stop going back to that "someday" thinking. You might not have tomorrow to start again, so today is your day. Make it count and make yourself proud.

Reflection
"The more reflective you are, the more effective you are."
~Hall and Simeral

- What has prevented you from going forward with changing your habits?

- What decision can you make today to make the change you need?

- How can you be sure to follow through with that decision?

Chapter 6- Believe in Yourself

"I have learned that champions aren't just born; champions can be made when they embrace and commit to life-changing positive habits."
~Lewis Howes

When I start working with my clients, the first thing we always do is begin addressing mindset because your mindset is so powerful. If you do not believe in yourself, nothing you want can happen. If you believe negative, you will attract negative. It is like that quote, "Whether you think you can or you think you can't, you are probably right." Everything begins in your mindset, and so it is important you approach each aspect of your life with a positive mindset.

If you want to reach your goals, your mind and self-care belong at the top of your to-do list. When you protect your health and wellbeing, you give yourself the strength you need to be successful. In order to begin this you first must begin with your mindset. As busy women, we wear many hats. We are mothers, sisters, wives, students, employees and even entrepreneurs. It can be easy to become overwhelmed and put yourself on the back burner. It is also easy to beat yourselves up in an effort to be perfect. The quickest way to burn out is to assume that you have to be perfect or that you will take care of you later.

Throughout my life, I have had BIG goals and I learned that unless I want to fail at all of them I have to be intentional about taking care of myself. In doing so I have been able to connect and live out my purpose without the overwhelm. I first began with addressing my mindset. It has been said that for every positive thought we have five negative thoughts. I had to be intentional about thinking positively. I did this through constantly affirming myself and being conscious of my goals. I would let myself know that even if I did not see it I had to believe it. I was very intentional about stopping the flaw focus, meaning I had to redirect my thoughts past my flaws. One of the things that hurts your ability to have more joy is focusing on your flaws. We all have them, but we are often hardest on ourselves. If your inner circle focuses on flaws it is time to adjust your circle. Likewise, if you are paying too much attention to your own flaws, then it's time to change your mindset. We should only be practicing love and self-acceptance each day.

The next thing I focused on was gratitude. It's easy to focus on the day-to-day stress and lose sight of the simple things that you're thankful for. When you reframe your thinking to encompass more positive thoughts, you will find gratitude more frequently. Make a list or keep a journal of all the good things in your life.

Review it each day. This will help you find peace and joy on a daily basis. You will see that your life is not made up of just negative moments. Your gratitude list can include ordinary things such as having a home, a bed, or breakfast every morning. The key is to focus on the areas of your life that make you feel happy. One way I do this is by asking myself, "What if I wake up tomorrow with ONLY the things I thanked God for yesterday?" It really makes me more appreciative of EVERYTHING.

One personal step I took to work and improve my mindset was making a happy board. A happy board is similar to a vision board, but a happy board is filled with things that make you happy – right now – rather than goals that you are working toward. This is something I look at weekly and more frequently if I am starting to lose my focus. You can make it on paper or design it online using programs such as Canva or even Pinterest. The key is to use the space to add things that bring joy to your life and help you rejuvenate when your mindset is in a dark place.

Finally, one thing I often share with my clients is the importance of forgiving themselves. You cannot experience happiness if you're constantly blaming yourself and making yourself feel awful. It's important to learn how to forgive yourself in order to have joy. Learn to let go of the guilt and shame that has built up in your life. Negative situations come up for everyone. Make a conscious effort to avoid dwelling on them. We will talk more about that in chapter nine.

One thing that I have learned is that if you make self-care automatic, you will create habits you can depend on to see you through major setbacks as well as minor irritations. Below are the nine strategies that I have used to incorporate self-care into my life.

1. **Think positive.** Studies show that optimists live longer and have stronger immune systems. Look on the bright side and count your blessings.
2. **Sleep well.** Sleep provides a time for restoration and rejuvenation. Go to bed and rise on a consistent schedule. Turn off the television and block out streetlights and noises if they are keeping you up at night.
3. **Manage stress.** Find relaxation practices that work for you. You might enjoy soaking in a warm bath or meditating in a quiet spot.

4. **Take frequent breaks.** Scheduling some downtime makes you more productive. Stand up and stretch when you are working at the office. Pause in between errands to drink a cup of tea and calm your mind.
5. **Delegate wisely.** Focus on the tasks that match your strengths. Try to transfer the rest of your responsibilities to others, whether that means hiring a housecleaner or trading assignments with a co-worker.
6. **Develop a hobby.** Fill your leisure time with meaningful activities. Creative pastimes can help you relax and feel accomplished.
7. **Be assertive.** Stand up for yourself. Ask for what you need tactfully and directly. Remember that you are worthy of respect and consideration.
8. **Stay connected.** Cultivate close relationships with family and friends. Make time in your schedule for family dinners and coffee dates. Invite a new colleague out to lunch. Call up a friend you haven't seen in a while so you can catch up.
9. **Seek inspiration.** Find something that motivates you. You might want to join a prayer group at your church or climb a mountain to admire the view.

Make yourself a priority and watch how your habits change.

Reflection
"The more reflective you are, the more effective you are."
~Hall and Simeral

- What is the biggest thing you need to conquer in your mind right now?

- How are you taking care of yourself?

- What is one self-care method that you can consistently implement in your life?

Chapter 7- Getting Accountability

"The people you surround yourself with influence your behaviors, so choose friends who have healthy habits."
~ Dan Buettner

It is so important to identify someone we are close to who will help push us in the right direction. You would call that person an accountability partner. An accountability partner will require you to take responsibility for what you are doing, and will also help you to stay true to your commitment. When I began my business, there were some habits that I displayed regularly that I knew would negatively affect my success. I liked to talk on the phone excessively. I don't know if you have tried it, but talking on the phone and writing books does not go hand in hand. Once I was aware that this habit was not going to be beneficial, I knew that I needed to make a change. The problem was I knew that I was not going to always be able to maintain the change by myself. I had to practice being intentional about changing and be consistent with it.

I decided that I would get business accountability partners. This felt risky to me because I knew I would have to be honest, but the big picture of being successful was much more important to me than the fear of what others would think. When I pinpointed the individuals that I trusted and knew would be helpful, I set up regular meeting times with them. We decided that we would meet bi-weekly to check on one another's progress. In business, it is easy to fall off because no one is checking on you. After all, it is your business, especially if you do not have a partner. Having people that I was accountable to was truly life changing. Every time I felt like I wanted to watch television or hop on the phone instead of writing or promoting on social media, I knew I would have to answer to my accountability partners. Knowing that I had to be accountable for my actions helped to redirect my steps. When I was forced to face those habits, it encouraged me to reflect on what I needed to change if I desired to be successful.

Having accountability partners really improved my progress and so I started to think of other ways I could increase my accountability. In my experience, I have noticed that if you hold yourself to a higher level of accountability, you are more likely to actually reach your goals. One of the things I did was download an app called STICKK. You can either use it to track habits you want to break or habits you want to develop. Every week, on a day that you choose, the app will alert you and ask you to update your progress. Having a little bit of accountability kept me focused on where I was going. With this app, there is a community of individuals who are working on breaking bad habits as well. Having this community influenced me in a way that made me not to want to let anyone down.

I also knew that hiring a coach would give me the momentum to reach my goals much quicker. When I set goals and intentions for the week, my coach holds me accountable and even gives me strategies to increase my success. Having that extra accountability when you are trying to break those habits is what is going to keep you on the path of success. Being accountable certainly requires you to be vulnerable. It requires you to share the habits you want to get rid of, which means you have to admit that you are flawed. Understand that you're not alone. Everybody is flawed. Every person has a habit that they want to get rid of. The fact that you are taking the first step in reading this book puts you light years beyond your peers.

When you surround yourself with successful people, you have no choice but to succeed as well. It goes back to the old saying "You are the average of the top five people you spend the most time with." It is imperative that you are conscious of the people you spend your time with. You want to make sure that you are surrounding yourself with people who will uplift you; those who will help you to break those habits. Recently, I was on the phone with a friend. I was on my way to pick up my daughter from daycare and mentioned that I wanted to have a milkshake after having a stressful day. I didn't intend to say it, and as a matter of fact, I had told her earlier that I wanted to limit my intake of sweets and ultimately get rid of them. My friend immediately checked me saying "Excuse me, you do not need to be going to get a milkshake. You just said you were trying to eliminate sweets." That was amazing to me. Technically, I didn't ask her to be an accountability partner, but I appreciated the fact that she remembered it enough to check me at that moment and pull me back into reality. She helped me remember that I was trying to get rid of that habit. This was a great example of why it's important to surround yourself with successful people who help you to stay on track.

Trying to identify an accountability partner can be challenging and can make you feel very vulnerable. It is normal to feel that way in the beginning. Do not let it stop you from giving it a try. You are human. Attempting to change habits all on your own can be tough. It is okay to reach out for extra support and encouragement along your journey. When you get to the other side it will make it that much sweeter!

Reflection
"The more reflective you are, the more effective you are."
~Hall and Simeral

- How will becoming accountable help you with breaking your habits?

- Who could you reach out to for more accountability?

- What do you need from an accountability partner?

Chapter 8 - Facing Your Fear
"Too many of us are not living our dreams because we are too busy living our fears."
~Les Brown

The thought of changing your lifestyle or your basic habits can cause a lot of fear. Although it is a very common life experience, fear is dangerous. When you are stuck in the cycle of fear, it can seem impossible to break free. Being stuck can make you feel like you will never have the opportunity to reach the other side where there is freedom, change and growth. There is an element of not knowing or realizing that other things exist. When I first set out to write my book, I gave myself many reasons why the idea was ridiculous. I decided that I wanted to hold onto the habits that were comfortable to me. Habits such as watching TV, talking on the phone and scrolling through social media were what I wanted to do. The dream I had of writing a book never died. Because the dream never died, I decided that I was going to need to make changes if I wanted to actually accomplish it.

I knew that if I wanted to change my life I needed to modify my daily activities. I revamped my schedule. I would go to work, come home and start writing. I fasted from social media, cut off my phone after a certain time and I was focused. After my book was published, so many things changed and it really transformed my life. When I look back on that process, I get frustrated with myself. I had allowed fear to paralyze me to the point where I was preventing my own success. This is why I tell people all of the time that fear is dangerous. We have so much potential living inside of us. The truth is, potential is nothing without action. We have to conquer the habits that prevent us from taking action on the things we need to do in order to reach our goals.

Fear is a natural part of life, but it can have a negative impact if you allow it to paralyze you. As a single mother, I love traveling with my girls, but it was not always like that. I would plan a trip and then cancel it because I would convince myself of all that could go wrong. Now that I LOVE traveling, it is frustrating to look back and think of all of the places and events we missed because of my fears.

Most fears are crippling and influence your decisions in negative ways. The more fears you have, the less freedom you enjoy.

Try these techniques to overcome your fears and to live freely:

1. **Become more aware.** There is a big world out there with a variety of perspectives. Yours might not be the best perspective. You

might believe that a fear of public speaking is very normal and justified, but is it? What is the worst that could happen if you make a mistake? No one is going to stone you.

2. **Determine why you're afraid.** What are the things that cause you to be afraid?

3. **Deal with your fears a little at a time.** For example, if you're afraid of public speaking, try giving a speech to your child, nephew, or niece. Next, trying giving a speech to a group of three. Build up your tolerance until you can speak to thousand.

Reflection
"The more reflective you are, the more effective you are."
~Hall and Simeral

- Take an inventory of your fears and make a list.

- Determine which fears are causing your life the most grief. Which fears do you spend the most time working around? Which are the most limiting?

- What have your fears cost you?

Chapter 9 - Give Grace

"Whatever we are waiting for - peace of mind, contentment, grace, the inner awareness of simple abundance - it will surely come to us, but only when we are ready to receive it with an open and grateful heart."
~Sarah Ban Breathnach

The next step in your process of forming and breaking habits is to give yourself grace. I do not know you personally, but I know sometimes it feels impossible for me to be graceful to myself. I struggle with needing things to be perfect and when I fail, it can be challenging to forgive myself. In that, way I can be my own worst enemy and I am sure you may struggle with that as well. As I mentioned before, we are all human. We all have habits that suck, which can eat us alive, that we regret, that we wish we did not do and that we wish we could overcome, but that is part of being human. Honestly, I am grateful for my habits because as I have to work through them, I become a stronger person. I gain the discipline I need which I can also apply later in life.

It has been said that it takes 21 days to break an old habit. Honestly, I have always questioned that number. Our habits are firmly ingrained in our minds and can take a ton of reprogramming to change. As I have been doing more research about habits, it appears that studies are highlighting that it takes more like 60 days to break a habit. I try not to focus so much on the number of days. I remember giving up sweets for 40 days for Lent. After that 40 days I thought I was cleared. The problem is that I fell right back into the habit because it was familiar. Once I fell off the bandwagon, I soon gave up because I felt like a total failure. I went from eating on pack of sweetarts to eating donuts, a milkshake, more candy and cookies all in the same week. What felt like a mistake seemed like an even bigger failure by the end of that week? What I came to learn was that I was not being fair to myself. I believed in the idea that since I was past my 21 days that I was in the clear. The reality is that I am still human and I have failure patterns that contributed to my embracing those habits. While I made one mistake, I had the chance to learn from it and make the change that I needed. What I did not do though was give myself grace. I beat myself up so badly that I subconsciously made it okay to continue down that negative spiral. In this experience, I learned the importance of giving myself grace.

Give yourself grace to make mistakes, give yourself grace when you fall off, and forgive yourself when things go wrong. When you give yourself grace, it helps to take the pressure off. The added pressure prevents you from being motivated. It is important that you acknowledge the habit, but do not judge yourself. We can be our own worst enemy because we are so quick to judge ourselves and say things that are negative and discouraging. In turn, the only thing you have done is internalized that negativity and made it more difficult to believe that you can break free from your habits. Choose to give yourself grace by lifting yourself up and saying things that acknowledge the mistake, but are motivating and encouraging. You can tell yourself that you messed up, but that you will try again. We are human and falling short is a part of life but it's not the end. You can begin again and be more successful than you know.

Grace is about acceptance, forgiveness and love. As hard and bitter as this pill is to swallow, grace heals you unlike anything else. There is no magic formula, but those who are open to receiving grace and those who practice self-compassion will tell you that grace begins to mold together the fractures.

For this chapter I did some research on grace and one person that I know extends much grace is God. God gave Adam a wife when he was alone. (Genesis 2:18). God clothed Adam and Eve after they sinned and realized they were naked. (Genesis 3:21). God provided hope of the coming of Jesus when he gave Adam and Eve the consequence for their sin. (Genesis 3:15 and Romans 16:20). God protected and gave grace to Cain, even after he had killed his brother. (Genesis 4:15). God saved Noah and his family when he destroyed the rest of the earth with a flood. (Genesis 6:17-18). This is all in the first book of the Bible! Imagine how much more grace was extended throughout the rest of the bible. If God can continue to provide us grace even until today, we have to learn to extend the same courtesy to ourselves.

Reflection
"The more reflective you are, the more effective you are."
~Hall and Simeral

- In what ways have, you tried to be perfect?

- Why is it important to give yourself grace?

- How can you be more kind to yourself and give yourself grace?

Chapter 10 - Visualize The Outcome

"Good habits are worth being fanatical about."
~John Irving

When working on changing habits, my favorite step is to visualize what that would both mean and look like. For example, you may decide that you don't want to go to Starbucks for the rest of the year. The question is, are you looking at the big picture? This would be asking yourself what your life would look like if you don't stop at Starbucks. Take a second to close your eyes and really visualize it. Envision it and make it feel real. You could change the verbiage to something more tangible: *If I don't drive to Starbucks, I'll have more money. I won't be late to work.* There are many things that could change in your life as a result of changing this habit. In the mornings you might have an extra five minutes to curl your hair or pick out new clothes. You may be more alert or lose the last five pounds you have desired to lose. When I think about it with my addiction to sweets, they can cost me in upwards of $50 a month. It's surprising to realize how those small things add up. I love milkshakes, cookies, cinnamon buns and other random junk food, but when I stopped to visualize what my life would look like, I knew it would change drastically. I recognized that I would have more energy. I would not have sugar crashes, which come as a result of needing real food and nutrients. I realized that I would probably save a ton of money because I would not be spending it on junk food. I would also save more time because I am not driving to these random places that I know have my favorite snacks.

The truth is, my sugar habit got completely out of control. It was challenging to think about getting rid of this particular habit. When I chose to visualize what changing that habit would mean for my life, it changed my entire perspective. Instantly it felt worthwhile. You will gain the momentum to push through when you really take a second to visualize what it is to accomplish breaking free of your habit. I often like to take it a step further and create a vision board of what my life will look like when I break that habit. My body was on point on my "sugar free" vision board! I posted that board and motivational quotes right on my pantry door. It stopped me dead in my tracks every time I wanted my favorite snacks. It reminded me of why I was implementing the change and the outcome I desired. When I added that visualization component to my habit changing process, it made it feel real and it strengthened my desire to meet that goal. **In completing research for this book, I** decided to look more in depth on the importance of visualization. Here are the main benefits to visualization:

- It helps relieve stress.
- Visualization improves your health.
- It increases the level of your happiness.
- It increases your self-confidence.

Reflection
"The more reflective you are, the more effective you are."
~Hall and Simeral

- Have you been honest with yourself about how this habit is currently playing out in your life?

- What will your life look like when you rid yourself of this habit or begin the new habit?

- How can you implement the practice of visualization to inspire you to make this change?

Chapter 11- Being Courageous

"In order to achieve success in any area of life you must be courageous enough to implement habits that will help you succeed."
~Nicolya

Just like the lion in the Wizard of Oz, you probably have more courage than you think. While you may find it difficult to ask a stranger to stop talking during a movie, you would rise to the occasion if a wicked witch threatened you and your friends. In real life, you could wait for a crisis that will bring out the lion in you or you can start now to practice habits that will build up your courage. Try these three steps that will help you to overcome the doubts and fears that hold you back from fulfilling your dreams.

Face Your Fears:

1. **Reframe the situation.** The words you choose to describe an event can have a profound effect on how you feel about it. View challenges as opportunities and try to avoid exaggerating negative consequences. When you are stuck in a long line, think of it as a chance to catch up on reading the news.

2. **Evaluate inaction.** It is natural to want to run away from the things that scare you, but avoidance comes at a high cost. You might lose a friend because you sidestep a sensitive conversation where you could work out your differences.

3. **Manage stress.** Maybe you are not even sure about the source of your fears. Dealing with daily stress reduces your anxiety levels. Find relaxation techniques that work for you such as meditation or listening to music.

4. **Seek support.** Asking for help can be a sign of courage. Reach out to loved ones or a professional counselor if you need help.

5. **Start small.** Major undertakings become less overwhelming when you break them down into parts that are more manageable. Work your way up to asking your boss for a

raise by being more assertive in situations where you have less at stake.

Strengthen Your Purpose:

1. **Dream big.** Courage expands your vision. Imagine what you would do if you could set aside any limiting beliefs. Find something that you value more than your pride or comfort.

2. **Clarify your goals.** To get tangible results, it is crucial to translate your vision into a practical plan of action. Identify exactly what you are going to do.

3. **Create a timeline.** You are more likely to stay on track if you decide what actions you will complete today or by the end of the month. Deadlines increase accountability.

4. **Keep a journal.** Put your plan into writing and post it somewhere where you can see it. That way it will stay fresh in your mind.

Build up Your Confidence:

1. **Think positive.** Focus on what you have to gain. Use your self-talk to give yourself reassurance and encouragement. Identify areas where you want to make changes, and be willing to laugh at yourself.

2. **Get organized.** Cleaning up your surroundings can make you feel more relaxed. Clear off your desk each evening and cut down on clutter at home.

3. **Come prepared.** Doing your homework helps you to place more trust in your abilities. Research a company before going

on a job interview or talk with a carpenter before tackling a home improvement project.

4. **Stay fit.** Caring for your health and wellbeing is one way to value yourself. Eat a balanced diet, exercise regularly, and get adequate sleep.

5. **List your accomplishments.** Boost your morale by reviewing your record of accomplishment. Your past victories prove that you can succeed at future tasks.

6. **Stretch your skills.** You will have more confidence in your abilities when you consistently work at increasing your competence. Take business courses online or study a foreign language.

Train yourself to be brave. Learn to master your fears and persist through challenges. Enjoying a more meaningful life is the ultimate reward of building up your courage.

Chapter 12 - Conclusion

"A change in bad habits leads to a change in life."
~Jenny Craig

Scientists believe that at least a third of our lives is lived on autopilot. This means that *one third* of the actions we take are not even consciously decided. The good news is that we do not have to let our habits control us any longer. We can get our lives back on track by learning to be in control of our habits.

Bad habits interrupt your life and prevent you from accomplishing your goals. They can also negatively influence your health both mentally and physically. Ultimately, bad habits waste your time and energy, preventing you from using that time and energy on much more valuable things.

While I certainly do not have all of the answers on how to break free of your habits for good, I have used this system and the strategies mentioned repeatedly. I have succeeded in reaching my goals by breaking those old habits and replacing them with healthy habits. It means nothing to recognize your habits and then refuse to do anything about them. You must first take heed to them, recognize the need for change and then be willing to implement a strategy that will give you the strength to rid yourself of the habits that are holding you back.

Breaking bad habits takes time, energy and effort, but mostly it takes perseverance. Most people who end up breaking their bad habits try and fail multiple times before they make it work. The key is they do not give up. You might not have success right away, but that does not mean you cannot have it at all. Keep pushing toward what you desire to achieve. Perseverance does pay off in time.

As I close out, I want you to remember that it is possible to change your habits to align with the desires you have for your life.

Now go and make the changes you need to live your dream....

Reflection
"The more reflective you are, the more effective you are."
~Hall and Simeral

- What are my biggest takeaways from this book?

- Why was this helpful?

- What can I begin implementing today?

Appendices

Takeaway Quote

"Sow a thought, and you reap an act;
Sow an act, and you reap a habit;
Sow a habit, and you reap a character;
Sow a character, and you reap a destiny."
— **Samuel Smiles**

Habit Affirmation

My habits lead to goal achievement.

My decisions determine my ability to achieve my goals. I practice habits that build me and make me successful.

I spend a lot of time reading because it produces knowledge and makes me conversant. Professional opportunities are more attainable when I am aware. Keeping abreast of the news allows me to prepare myself for global change.

Exercise clears my mind and allows me to focus on work. When I release the stress of yesterday, I am able to concentrate on resolving the challenges of today.

I know that my diet is a crucial part of achieving my fitness goals. Planning meals on the weekend allows me to stay on track towards fitness. It prevents me from falling into the trap of eating unhealthy meals.

Balance is essential to coping with competing aspects of my life. Although I like to get things done quickly, I am diligent about making time for relaxation.

A body that is relaxed feels ready to take on the world.

Scheduling time for study is easy for me because I focus on my upcoming graduation day. Zoning in on the mission at hand ignites the desire to put first things first.

Today, I practice positive habits that help me achieve my goals. I realize that taking this approach results in less difficulty in my life. Goals are more straightforward and simpler to achieve when I put myself in the position to achieve them.

Self-Reflection Questions:

1. How do I keep myself from developing unhealthy habits?

2. Where do I turn when I need guidance on how to solve a challenging situation?

3. What are some of the biggest challenges that I have been able to overcome?

Habit Breaking Countdown
"Great character is not developed through ease and convenience but through doing NOW what needs to be done no matter how difficult it."

We all have negative habits that take away from our success. In this template, you will identify a habit that you want to break over the next thirty days. Take time to reflect on the habit. The trouble that it has caused identify a plan to break myself of this habit. On the table, identify the steps you took each day to avoid engaging in your habit! At the end of the thirty days, reflect on your progress. I have included three different templates for the top three habits that need to be broken TODAY!

Habit Breaking Countdown

I will break/start the habit of

Why do I want to break this habit?

What is my plan to break this habit for good?

Who will keep me accountable?

This is important to me because

When I want to give up, I will

If I am successful at riding myself of this habit, what will my reward be?

Countdown the days to success

Day 1	
Day 2	
Day 3	
Day 4	
Day 5	
Day 6	
Day 7	
Day 8	
Day 9	
Day 10	
Day 11	
Day 12	
Day 13	
Day 14	
Day 15	

Day 16	
Day 17	
Day 18	
Day 19	
Day 20	
Day 21	
Day 22	
Day 23	
Day 24	
Day 25	
Day 26	
Day 27	
Day 28	
Day 29	
Day 30	

How did I do?

Habit Breaking Countdown

I will break/start the habit of

Why do I want to break this habit?

What is my plan to break this habit for good?

Who will keep me accountable?

This is important to me because

When I want to give up, I will

If I am successful at riding myself of this habit, what will my reward be?

Countdown the days to success

Day 1	
Day 2	
Day 3	
Day 4	
Day 5	
Day 6	
Day 7	
Day 8	
Day 9	
Day 10	
Day 11	
Day 12	
Day 13	
Day 14	
Day 15	

Day 16	
Day 17	
Day 18	
Day 19	
Day 20	
Day 21	
Day 22	
Day 23	
Day 24	
Day 25	
Day 26	
Day 27	
Day 28	
Day 29	
Day 30	

How did I do?

Habit Breaking Countdown

I will break/start the habit of

Why do I want to break this habit?

What is my plan to break this habit for good?

Who will keep me accountable?

This is important to me because

When I want to give up, I will

If I am successful at riding myself of this habit, what will my reward be?

Countdown the days to success

Day 1	
Day 2	
Day 3	
Day 4	
Day 5	
Day 6	
Day 7	
Day 8	
Day 9	
Day 10	
Day 11	
Day 12	
Day 13	
Day 14	
Day 15	

Day 16	
Day 17	
Day 18	
Day 19	
Day 20	
Day 21	
Day 22	
Day 23	
Day 24	
Day 25	
Day 26	
Day 27	
Day 28	
Day 29	
Day 30	

How did I do?

DAILY HABIT TRACKER
"We are what we repeatedly do."

    This is a weekly habit tracker for the next month, which will allow you to keep track of how many times you are participating in healthy habits leading you closer to your goals. Identify five daily habits that will push you closer to your goals. At the end of each week, be sure to reflect on your experiences and challenges and make a plan for success for the following week. After trying it for a month, work on implementing them daily for the next three months. Some examples of habits that I implemented daily included; saying affirmations, reading, working out, and participating in my daily power hour. I also did a lot of self-care activities because the truth is, if you're not fueling your body you will not have the energy you need to be successful. You can consider setting healthy habits on this tracker such as drinking 64 ounces of water, getting 8 hours of sleep or working out. These are just some suggestions please make sure you are identifying habits that you also believe will help you on your journey to success. When you first begin, you may not be implementing these habits daily. The goal is that you are practicing these healthy habits with more and more frequency until they become normal habits.

Week 1

New Habit	SUN	MON	TUES	WED	THURS	FRI	SAT

Weekly Reflection:

Week 2

New Habit	SUN	MON	TUES	WED	THURS	FRI	SAT

Weekly Reflection:

Week 3

New Habit	SUN	MON	TUES	WED	THURS	FRI	SAT

Weekly Reflection:

Week 4

New Habit	SUN	MON	TUES	WED	THURS	FRI	SAT

Weekly Reflection:

About Nicolya

Nicolya Williams is the type of woman who pursues her goals with passion and determination. She is dedicated to helping other women conquer their chaos and reach their goals. Nicolya is a personal development coach, radio host, best-selling author, and blogger for women. Nicolya graduated from The Ohio State University (B.A., Psychology) and obtained her M.Ed. from the University of Dayton with a focus on Clinical Counseling and School Counseling. She is currently a doctoral student with a focus on Transformational Leadership. Nicolya holds a Coach Practitioner certificate and is licensed as both a Community Counselor and School Counselor, with a Chemical Dependency Counselor Assistant license.

Nicolya is a lifelong learner who strives to continue her personal growth through reading and interacting with her social and spiritual community. She is an avid reader and is devoted to building up her own strong women; her daughters, Kaelyn and Kamryn. Nicolya is committed to creating a space for women to be heard and successful! You can connect with Nicolya at www.nicolyawilliams.com or on all social media platforms via @NicolyaWilliams. You can with Nicolya at www.nicolyawilliams.com or on all social media platforms via @NicolyaWilliams. You can also check out Nicolya's other books on Amazon!

Clarity Cove Publishing
~We publish books the world needs~

Clarity Cove Publishing was created by Nicolya Williams. Clarity Cove Publishing connects with powerful, determined and driven women to help them turn their message into their masterpiece. We offer publishing services, writing assistance, marketing strategies and much more. Our vision is to foster creativity, encourage risk taking and increase clarity around your book writing goals. Our authors have an opportunity to get their message out into the masses without losing their authenticity in the process.

To inquire about publishing with us or getting support along your publishing journey reach out to us at
http://www.nicolyawilliams.com/clarity-cove-publishing/
or email at claritycove@nicolyawilliams.com

www.ingramcontent.com/pod-product-compliance
Lightning Source LLC
Chambersburg PA
CBHW071734040426
42446CB00012B/2355